SCHOMBURG

The Man Who Built a Library

Carole Boston Weatherford

illustrated by Eric Velasquez

CANDLEWICK PRESS

Be curious. Be determined. Be proud.

Curiosity is the seed of discovery. Discovery is the root of progress.

C. B. W.

Para Arturo Alfonso Schomburg. Gracias, maestro.

E. V.

Thank you to the Schomburg Center for its help and continued support, and thanks to Sheena Bouchét Simmons from Harlem, USA, for the inspiration to do a book on Schomburg. — E. V.

Candlewick Press, 99 Dover Street, Somerville, Massachusetts 02144. visit us at www.candlewick.com.

Printed in Shenzhen, Guangdong, China. 20 21 22 23 24 CCP 10 9 8 7 6 5

The American Negro must remake his past in order to make his future. . . . History must restore what slavery took away.

—Arturo Schomburg

PROLOGUE: BIBLIOPHILE

Arturo Schomburg was more than a book lover,
more than a mailroom clerk at Bankers Trust,
where he supervised eleven white men,
unheard-of authority for a black man at the time.
He recognized early on that history was not history
unless it was complete from all angles.
Like a detective, he hunted for clues and found facts
affirming the role of African descendants
in building nations and shaping cultures.
Fellow book collector Arthur Spingarn noted
　　that Arturo would *approach*
an immense pile of apparently worthless material
and unerringly find . . . one or two treasures
which would have been lost to a less inspired collector.
Arturo believed that those facts, once unearthed,
would speak loud and clear in halls of knowledge,
daring another teacher to tell a black child
that *the Negro has no history.* Time and again,
through print, music, and art, Schomburg proved otherwise.
On his lifelong quest, he was not just collecting rarities;
he was correcting history for generations to come.
He wanted the facts to reach the community
and boys and girls in classrooms to teach them
that black heritage knows no national boundaries.
And today, the Harlem library bearing Schomburg's name
boasts more than ten million items, a beacon
for scholars all over the world, bringing to light
past glories that Arturo always knew existed.

◆

FIFTH GRADE

Arturo Schomburg was born with a sense of wonder.
As a boy in Puerto Rico, he shadowed *tabaqueros,*
    cigar workers.
These men pooled money to pay *el lector*
to read aloud in the factory:
newspapers, novels, speeches, and politics.
Arturo took in the scent of cured tobacco
and the sound of the reader's voice.
Thus, Arturo not only learned his ABCs
but also to love the written word.

So when his fifth-grade teacher
told him that Africa's sons and daughters
had no history, no heroes worth noting,
did the twinkle leave Arturo's eyes?
Did he slouch his shoulders, hang his head low,
and look to the ground rather than to the horizon?

No. His people must have contributed something
over the centuries, history that teachers did not teach.
Until they did, schoolchildren like Arturo
would not learn of their own heritage,
ignorance shackling them like chains.
After that teacher dismissed his people's past,
did the twinkle leave Arturo's eyes
like a candle blown out in the dark?
No, the twinkle never left. It grew into a spark.

◆

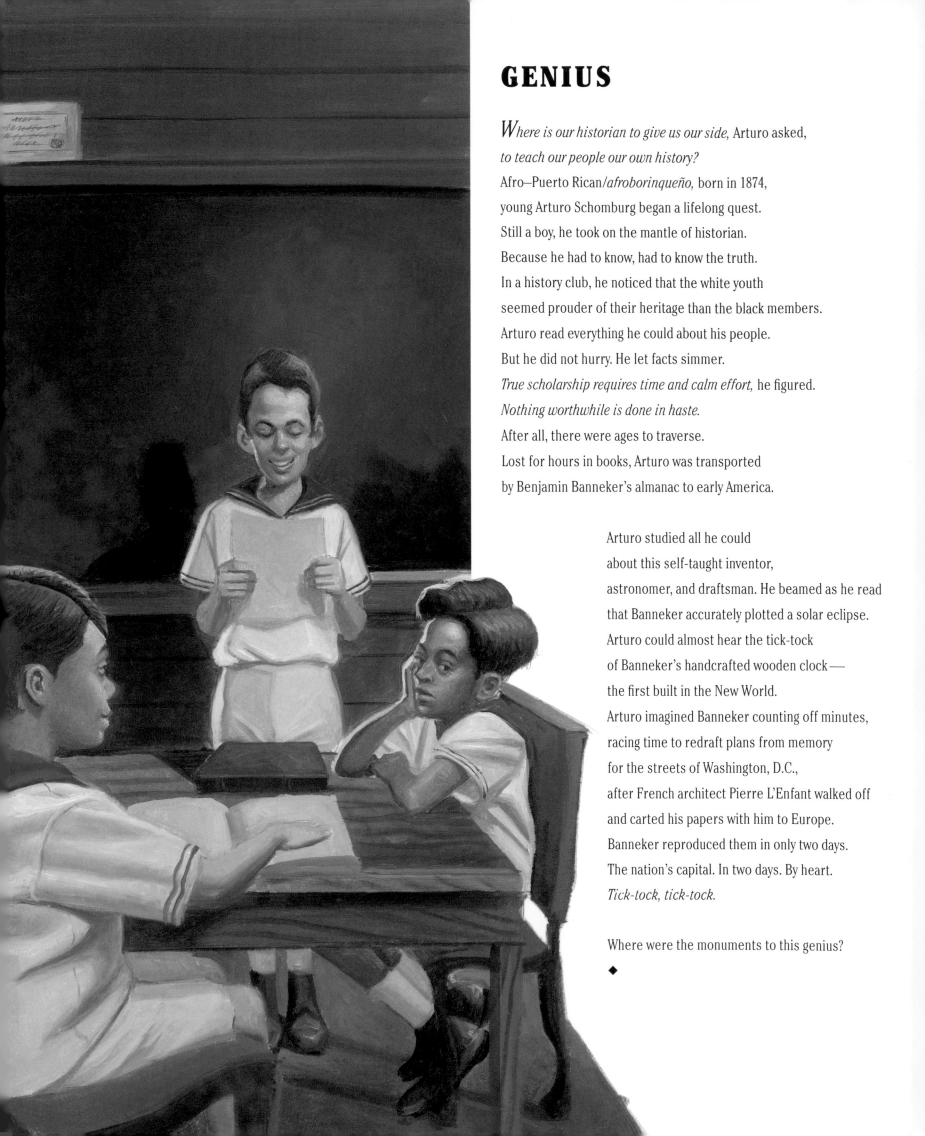

GENIUS

Where is our historian to give us our side, Arturo asked,
to teach our people our own history?
Afro–Puerto Rican/*afroborinqueño,* born in 1874,
young Arturo Schomburg began a lifelong quest.
Still a boy, he took on the mantle of historian.
Because he had to know, had to know the truth.
In a history club, he noticed that the white youth
seemed prouder of their heritage than the black members.
Arturo read everything he could about his people.
But he did not hurry. He let facts simmer.
True scholarship requires time and calm effort, he figured.
Nothing worthwhile is done in haste.
After all, there were ages to traverse.
Lost for hours in books, Arturo was transported
by Benjamin Banneker's almanac to early America.

Arturo studied all he could
about this self-taught inventor,
astronomer, and draftsman. He beamed as he read
that Banneker accurately plotted a solar eclipse.
Arturo could almost hear the tick-tock
of Banneker's handcrafted wooden clock—
the first built in the New World.
Arturo imagined Banneker counting off minutes,
racing time to redraft plans from memory
for the streets of Washington, D.C.,
after French architect Pierre L'Enfant walked off
and carted his papers with him to Europe.
Banneker reproduced them in only two days.
The nation's capital. In two days. By heart.
Tick-tock, tick-tock.

Where were the monuments to this genius?

◆

EL INMIGRANTE/
THE IMMIGRANT

When seventeen-year-old Arturo Schomburg
immigrated to New York from Puerto Rico in 1891,
he carried with him letters of introduction
from cigar makers and from José González Font,
who owned a printing press in San Juan
where Arturo had worked as a typographer.
Arturo presented the letters to Flor Baerga,
an amateur book collector
and staunch opponent of Spanish colonial rule.
Arturo perused Baerga's photos and clippings
about New York's Puerto Rican community
and soon found the local *tabaqueros*.
This time, he lived among them,
sharing their activism and their allegiance
to Cuban and Puerto Rican independence from Spain.
In support of *la causa*/the cause,
Arturo joined political groups
such as Las Dos Antillas/The Two Antilles

and wrote letters to the editor of the newspaper *Patria*
under the pen name Guarionex.

Newly arrived, Arturo sought to better himself,
giving Spanish lessons while learning English
in night school. Drawn to medicine and law,
he pursued neither because, as the story goes,
his official school records were lost in a fire.
Not even a letter from a former teacher
was sufficient proof of his formal education.
Kindergarten was all that could be documented.
So Arturo set aside dreams of a profession
and toiled as a messenger and clerk at the law firm
that was seeking to protect Johnson and Johnson's use
of the red cross logo on its products.
For that case, Arturo indexed and memorized
thousands of pages of testimony—
his recall of detail extraordinary.

◆

THE BOOK HUNTING BUG

I wanted to find out, said Arturo Schomburg,
what my own racial group had contributed.
He could not get his hands on enough books.
His curiosity about Africana — insatiable.
Arturo had what he called the *book hunting disease.*
No one volume told the whole story,
and no library specialized in the subject.

So he haunted rare book stores,
poring over fragile pamphlets with torn covers
and leather books with paper mites between pages.
Most of what he bought early on came cheap
because white collectors considered it junk.
Still, what he hunted was not easy to find.
But Arturo knew what clues and markers to look for.
Now and then, he happened upon a prize.

In Phillis Wheatley, the first African American
and third American woman
to have a book of poems published,
Arturo found not only a devotion to God and country
but also a biography as remarkable as her verse.
Captured at age seven in West Africa and named Phillis
after the slave ship on which she was cargo,
she was sold to John Wheatley but was sickly
and thus never trained as his wife's servant.
Poor in health but rich in a rare brilliance,
Phillis quickly mastered English and read the Bible.
She studied religion and the classics
and spoke several languages fluently.

But Phillis was most phenomenal as a poet.
If only Arturo could have been a gull
swooping and crooning above the waves
as Phillis crossed the Atlantic a second time,
bound for London to promote her book —
Poems on Various Subjects, Religious and Moral — in 1773.
If only that same year Arturo could have witnessed
that stroke of the pen granting Phillis her freedom.
If only Arturo could have looked over her shoulder,
seen her penning that praise poem
to George Washington during the Revolution.
Although she offered subscriptions
for a second book, her final manuscript
was never published or found.
If only, thought Arturo, *I could find that.*

◆

1773

FREDERICK DOUGLASS

As Arturo fanned the pages of Frederick Douglass's narrative,
it was as if a breeze carried him to the riverfront plantation
where sailboats first defined freedom for young Frederick.
Like Arturo, Frederick loved the written word.
He even broke the law against slaves learning to read.
As Frederick escaped bondage, Arturo followed his trail
from Maryland all the way to Massachusetts.
And when Douglass roared against slavery,
his speeches —*agitate! agitate! agitate!*—
awoke Arturo to the power of the pen.
With that aim, Douglass had rallied the abolitionist cause,
winning pledges of support and thunderous applause.
Arturo scanned Douglass's anti-slavery newspaper,
The North Star. The publication's motto rang true:

RIGHT IS OF NO SEX — TRUTH IS OF NO COLOR —

GOD IS THE FATHER OF US ALL, AND ALL MEN ARE BRETHREN.

Ten thousand volumes could not better define democracy.
A printer's helper as a teen, Arturo imagined Douglass
setting metal type and cranking the letterpress.
A tall man with deep-set eyes and a long woolly mane,
Douglass went on to become the U.S. minister to Haiti.
In his later years, he bought Cedar Hill, an estate
in Washington's Anacostia section, where he was deemed a sage.
Frederick's name, thought Arturo, in every archive should reside.
The words that Douglass wrote would keep his memory alive.

◆

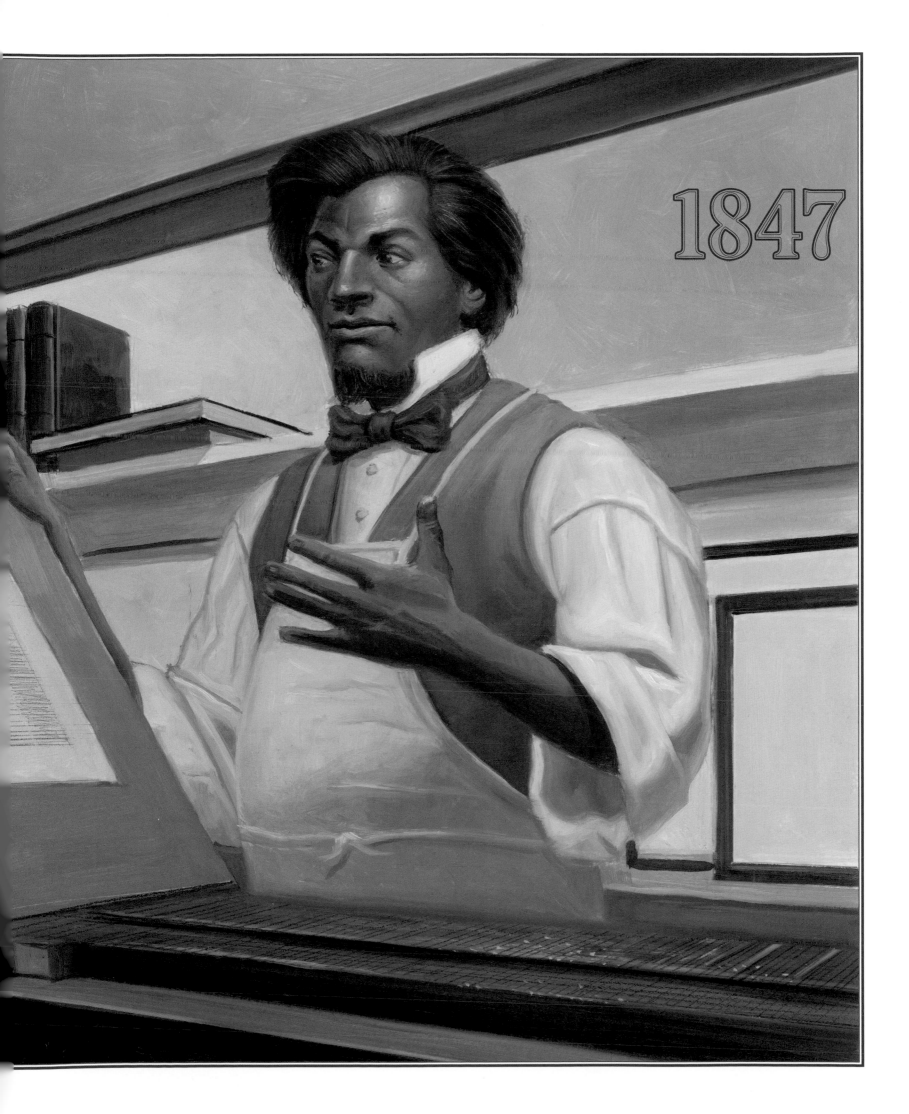

REVOLUTIONARIES

As Schomburg's search went on, he bought not only books
but also art, letters, prints, and rare African cameos.
His was a war to combat ignorance and shatter lies.
He needed an arsenal for that.
From the past, Arturo enlisted an army of exemplars.
His boyhood hero was Toussaint Louverture,
leader of the revolt that liberated slaves in Haiti.
Later, Arturo purchased military orders signed
by Louverture himself. A freed slave
with property and money, he risked all
to join a slave revolt. Just a generation
after American independence, Louverture
led a revolution that lasted twelve years
and cost thousands of lives. His troops fought off
first the French, then the British, and finally
the Spanish before victory was won
and a black republic born. Haiti.

For colonies and countries founded on slavery,
the Haitian revolution was a hurricane.
Whispers of Louverture's name
made slaveholders shudder.

1804

Contrary to popular belief, slaves did rise up —
and not just in the glorious liberation of Haiti.
Arturo eventually traced the roots of rebellion
to early America.
He read the radical pamphlet that David Walker,
a free black merchant, published in 1829:
An Appeal to the Colored Citizens of the World,
calling for slaves to rise up,
a fiery tract that was banned in its day.
Arturo studied the 1839 mutiny on the slave ship *Amistad*
and the court case that followed.
Some states soon outlawed anti-slavery literature
and forbade blacks from learning to read.
What did slaveholders fear?
In South Carolina and Virginia,
Denmark Vesey and Gabriel Prosser
planned uprisings. And in Virginia, Nat Turner
carried out his vision. His 1831 insurrection
brought together seventy blacks, slave and free,
and left fifty-seven whites dead.

Arturo breathed in his heroes' brave words.
In his way, Schomburg was a revolutionary, too.

◆

THREE ELIZABETHS

Arturo first married in 1895, the same year
he adopted the English version of his name —
Arthur. Elizabeth Hatcher of Staunton, Virginia,
was his bride. She died young, leaving her husband
to raise two sons, Maximo Gomez and Kingsley Guarionex;
a third, Arturo Alfonso Jr., died in infancy.

His second wife was Elizabeth Morrow Taylor,
also from Virginia. From their union
came two more children: Reginald Stanfield
and Nathaniel José. Both boys lived in Virginia
with their half brothers and their mother's mother.
It was common then for parents who worked in cities
to send their children off to be raised by kin.
On visits to the South, Arturo bristled at the color line.

When the second Elizabeth passed on,
he married another — Elizabeth Green.
They were blessed with three children:
Fernando, Dolores Marie, and Plácido Carlos.
Despite their Spanish names, Schomburg wouldn't let
    his offspring
learn his native tongue. They were Americans.

◆

WHITEWASH

In his quest for black glory, Arturo Schomburg navigated
a maze of misinformation that stripped Africans' humanity
and branded them as *less than* to justify slavery.
The system was based on skin color superiority and inferiority,
and was necessary, argued aristocrats, to build fortunes
   and empires.
Arturo suspected a conspiracy of fraud
that aimed to erase all African history but bondage.
Arturo saw that the historical record was colorblind
only when that best served greedy motives.
So when genius was black, skin color was left out.
But Schomburg chased the truth and turned up icons
whose African heritage had been whitewashed.

Arturo found African roots in the family tree
of artist, ornithologist, and naturalist John James Audubon.
His masterpiece was the book *Birds of America.*
With watercolors, pastel crayons, charcoal, and pencils,
he depicted North American birds in stunning lifelike poses.
Yet for all Audubon's fame, there was rarely mention
that he was born to a French plantation owner
and a Creole chambermaid.

As a boy, Arturo read *The Three Musketeers.*
I used to lose myself in that book, he later wrote,
and think I was fighting with Athos, Porthos and Aramis.
He memorized their motto: *All for one, one for all.*
But he had no inkling that the author,
Frenchman Alexandre Dumas, was descended from slaves.
Why had Arturo not learned that as a child?

1827

1833

Arturo discovered that Russia had its black star too,
the great poet Alexander Pushkin,
the father of that country's modern literature,
his first work published when he was just fifteen.
His great-grandfather was Abram Gannibal,
who was kidnapped as a child in Central Africa,
served in the court of Peter the Great,
and rose to become a general and an aristocrat himself.
No wonder Pushkin was famed for fighting duels.

Even German composer Ludwig van Beethoven
had ties to Africa. He was often described
as dark, a mulatto, or a Moor. His mother
was said to be a Moor — North African.
Gifted beyond belief, Beethoven
still composed after he'd lost his hearing.
How could this maestro's African heritage
    have been muted?

How could Arturo ever behold
Beethoven's Fifth Symphony
without hearing Africa drumming?

◆

1776

SEAFARING

Arturo Schomburg was becoming quite the collector.
He nabbed two volumes by Paul Cuffee,
an early American whaler, shipbuilder, and maritime trader
whose fleet sailed the United States Atlantic coast,
to the Caribbean, and to Europe.

On ships he'd built, Cuffee and his crew
whaled in the waters of the Atlantic.
This was dirty and dangerous work, but necessary.
First harpoons flew, and later blubber was rendered
into whale oil for lamps to light growing cities.

Paul Cuffee was one of the richest black men
in early America. He could afford to speak his mind.
Cuffee wrote a petition that free blacks
should be able to vote since they paid taxes.
And he was the first to float the back-to-Africa idea.

He could see free blacks and freed slaves settling
in Sierra Leone someday. Cuffee sailed there, set foot
on West African soil to judge if his new society might root.
At the White House, he reported that his dream —
to send one vessel to Africa each year — held promise.

In Cuffee, Arturo found a forerunner to Marcus Garvey,
the Harlem Renaissance leader who preached black pride,
self-help, and, like Cuffee a century earlier, a return to Africa.
In the 1920s, Arturo supported Garvey, his newspaper
Negro World, and his Black Star steamship line.

As the Garveyites paraded down Harlem's 125th Street
in plumed hats and tasseled, brass-buttoned uniforms,
did Paul Cuffee's voyages cross Arturo's mind?

◆

BLOODHOUND

Though a mailroom clerk at a bank by day,
Arturo rubbed shoulders with Alain Locke,
dubbed the Father of the Harlem Renaissance.
And he corresponded with Booker T. Washington,
founder of Tuskegee Institute, and W. E. B. Du Bois,
an Atlanta University professor and the first African American
to earn a doctorate from Harvard. The two disagreed
about whether to push for social or economic progress,
but they agreed that black history could be a bridge.

Arturo's acquaintances were a "Who's Who"
of the Harlem Renaissance. He was invited
to the first meeting of an informal guild of young black writers.
Poets Countee Cullen and Langston Hughes
    were members.
So was novelist and poet Jessie Redmon Fauset,
an editor of the NAACP magazine, *The Crisis,*
and of the African-American children's magazine,
The Brownies' Book. These writers joined Arna Bontemps,
Georgia Douglas Johnson, and artist Aaron Douglas
in asking Arturo to hunt for historic references that could water
the seeds of creative and scholarly endeavors.
His collection, fertile soil for growing black pride.
When it came to digging up rare finds and obscure facts,
Arturo had what poet Claude McKay called a *bloodhound's nose.*
Arturo loaned not only books to students, artists, and writers;
he also lent interpretations, insights, and sometimes cash.
With booklists full of texts that Schomburg found,
his friends mined blackness and broke new ground.

HOME

Busy, always busy, said Fernando of his father,
Arturo Schomburg. He was gone — traveling
on lecture tours or collecting missions —
for what seemed like eight months each year.
And when he was home in Brooklyn, he was out
most evenings for club and lodge meetings.
His visiting children lived among the countless books
in his collection. His only daughter, Dolores,
greeted artists and scholars who came by to view
his growing library. Arturo's wife, Elizabeth,
fought to carve out living space for the family,
but that was a losing battle. Her efforts
to clean his desk, also in vain. When she cleared
the clutter to dust, he complained
that important references were misplaced.
She finally left well enough alone.

◆

WRITER AND RESEARCHER

Arturo Schomburg aimed to prove Africans' place
in world history. In Harlem, he joined the Men's Sunday Club,
which grew into the Negro Society for Historical Research.
The society sponsored lectures and galas and, in its first year,
amassed more than three hundred books and manuscripts.
Arturo stored that collection at his home, alongside his own.

He was also president of the American Negro Academy
and grand secretary of the all-black Prince Hall Grand Masonic Lodge.
And he served on the committee to start a Negro division
at the Harlem branch of the New York Public Library.
Civic-minded but no social climber, he skipped
the famed parties of the Roaring Twenties Jazz Age.
Arturo preferred leafing through history to dancing the lindy hop.

With a busy schedule of lectures and meetings,
it's a wonder he had time for research or writing.
Arturo's articles, essays, and letters to the editor
shared what he had learned—facts kept in darkness far too long.
He profiled eighteenth-century composer
　　Chevalier de Saint-Georges.
A French knight known as the black Mozart,
Saint-Georges was a song to Arturo's heart.

He also wrote of gladiators, military leaders, and majesty.
One article tells of a huge pearl found by an African slave
on an island in the Gulf of Panama. The jewel
adorned Spanish queens until Napoleon's brother
took it to France. Sold to a British duke,
the pearl was lost in Buckingham Palace
and Windsor Castle but was recovered each time.
The gem's fabled past earned it the name
　　La Peregrina/The Wanderer.

Arturo's research pulled him along the triangular trade route,
just as surely as wind, currents, and greed carried supplies
from Europe to Africa to barter for slaves
and took captive Africans to American colonies
to grow sugarcane that would be distilled into rum
　　to be sold in Europe.
Through the pages of history, Arturo toured the diaspora.
His sense of Africana transcended national boundaries.
Heritage for him was braided from many threads.

Arturo's most important article was for *Survey Graphic.*
"The Negro Digs Up His Past" ran in a special issue,
Harlem: Mecca of the New Negro.
On the contents page, Arturo is listed
among other contributors—scholars and creative geniuses.
Schomburg's words give voice to the ancestors.
Their pigment flowed through his pen.

◆

SOLD

Rumor has it that Schomburg's wife put her foot down:
Either his books or their family must go. Only a threat like that
could make him part with his prizes.
There were bookshelves filled with books all over the house,
a family member said, *even in the bathroom.*
The books were carefully cataloged,
inventoried in Arturo's head,
and arranged by size and color of binding.
But Arturo's library had outgrown private hands.
He had turned down a very handsome offer
because the collection deserved a wider audience.
Arturo had already lent items to libraries
and staged exhibitions for schools and community groups.
He approached the New York Public Library,
but it lacked funds to purchase his vast holdings.
So the Carnegie Corporation bought the entire lot
for $10,000 and in 1926 donated it to the library.

If Harlem was the heart of African-American culture,
the 135th Street branch of the New York Public Library was the mind.
If the library were a university, its alumni would include
the Harlem Renaissance figures who lost themselves
amid its stacks and wrote in a quiet room downstairs.
Schomburg's collection, which one newspaper called *matchless,*
was housed on the third floor and would become
the cornerstone of the Division of Negro History,
    Literature and Prints.
It included more than five thousand books,
several thousand pamphlets, plus priceless prints and papers —
among them, an autographed first edition of poems
by Phillis Wheatley, the brilliant slave girl.
There were handwritten poems by Paul Laurence Dunbar,
letters of heroic general Toussaint Louverture,
speeches of slave-turned-statesman Frederick Douglass,
Benjamin Banneker's early American *Almanack,*
and a 1573 book of poems by Spaniard Juan Latino,
perhaps the first printed book by a black person.

◆

31

FISK UNIVERSITY

Arturo Schomburg studied the past,

but he did not dwell in it. Quite the opposite.

His mission looked to the future.

I am proud, said Schomburg, *to be able to do something*

that may mean inspiration for the youth of my race.

After a decade of headaches and nosebleeds,

Arturo retired in 1929 from his job at Bankers Trust.

But he did not rest. He spent more time

writing and researching and tending the collection

at the 135th Street Library.

On the strength of his reputation as a bibliophile,

Arturo was invited to Nashville in 1931 to found

Fisk University Library's Negro Collection.

By 1932, he had added four thousand volumes to the

library's holdings.

Lincoln's bible was the centerpiece.

When Arturo first held it, he thought of the free blacks

from Baltimore who had presented the hefty book

to the president during the Civil War.

That Bible was a priceless treasure,

but Arturo did not want black heritage behind glass.

He wanted his research to reach students.

So he told professors what to teach:

Include the practical history of the Negro race

from the dawn of civilization to the present time.

Then young blacks would hold their heads high

and view themselves as anyone's equal.

DOCTOR

After a year at Fisk University in Tennessee,
Arturo Schomburg returned to New York.
At the public library's 135th Street branch,
his treasures were now the core
of the Division of Negro History, Literature and Prints.
Arturo became the guardian of his collection.
His peculiar method of shelving books
arranged them by size and color, like a bouquet.
In fact, he fired a new librarian
for using the standard Dewey Decimal System.

The historical figures he unearthed still spoke to him.
Tell our stories, proclaim our glories.
From his perch on the library's third floor,
Arturo guided researchers, spoke at afternoon teas,
and used his own funds to enlarge the collection.
Among his gifts, *African Venus* and *Saïd Abdullah,*
classic bronzes by French sculptor
    Charles Henri Joseph Cordier.
Bought in Paris, both pieces had shown in the Louvre
in the 1860s. At $50, the stunning pair were a steal.
Arturo was not wealthy, but he used the money
from the sale of his collection to build on it.

When an item was over his budget,
he was not ashamed to appeal to friends for funds.
He asked a fellow book collector to donate
a bronze and marble bust of Shakespearean character
Othello, a Moorish general, to put on display.
Arturo organized exhibitions about Russian literary giant
Alexander Pushkin and black Shakespearean actor Ira Aldridge.
"Our Pioneers," Arturo's weekly column
for the *Amsterdam News,* was read all over Harlem.
The library staff called Arturo "Doctor Schomburg."
The home-grown historian had earned that honor.

◆

ART

In etchings, prints, paintings, and sculpture,
Arturo Schomburg saw not just art
but also an opportunity to offer visible proof
of the talent and accomplishments of
    African descendants.
The eye, he supposed, would refute the lie.
Arturo was drawn to works showing black subjects
regardless of the artist's skin color
and to works created by black artists
regardless of subject matter.
Whether he was collecting the work of Harlem Renaissance painters
such as Aaron Douglas and Lois Mailou Jones,
sculptors like Charles Henri Joseph Cordier
or Spanish Baroque artists like Sebastián Gómez
and Juan de Pareja, Arturo embraced
and pursued art with the same passion
and persistence that he did book buying.
Art, he thought, might reach those
who would never read a rare book.

◆

SPAIN

Arturo Schomburg had gained respect from Harlem's intellects,
but he had yet to trace his own roots —
African, Spanish, and Taino Indian —
from the Caribbean to Europe and Africa.
So he voyaged across the Atlantic,
not to collect but to connect the dots.
I depart now, he said, *on a mission of love*
  to recapture my lost heritage.
He mined libraries, museums, and rare book stores
for Spain's link in the chain of slavery.
He beheld masterworks painted by African hands
and marveled at palaces and mosques built
by the Arab and African Muslims who ruled Spain
  for eight hundred years.
These scenes and canvases, Arturo filed in his mind's eye.
Touring Spain, France, Germany, and England
did not produce answers to all his questions,
but Arturo had more than enough facts to take home.
This was Schomburg's only trip to Europe
and the farthest he would ever travel.
No distance was too great to set history straight.

◆

THE ISLANDS

Arturo Alfonso Schomburg may have felt kinship
with African Americans and their cause of equality
and even worked to build pride among them.
He may have adopted the Anglicized version of his name —
Arthur — and insisted that his children speak only English
and not Spanish, his own mother tongue.
But he never lost his love for the Caribbean
or his longing for Puerto Rico, the island of his birth.
His research took him back to the Caribbean
    and to Latin America:
Haiti, the Dominican Republic, Panama, and Cuba.

Arturo was a bridge between great minds in Havana
and Harlem. In 1932 he met Cuban poet Nicolás Guillén
and with Club Atenas, a group of writers, artists,
    and scholars
who celebrated Cuba's rich and colorful cultural heritage.
Most of Arturo's publications focused on the
    Caribbean and Spain;
his first, an article on the Haitian revolution and independence.
At the 135th Street Library in Harlem,
Arturo organized exhibitions of Cuban folklore and literature.
But despite his yearnings, he never visited Puerto Rico after 1909.

◆

EPITAPH:
1938

If this proverb
A book is like a garden carried in a pocket
is true, then Arturo Alfonso Schomburg,
the historian and book collector,
had a green thumb and a harvest of pride.
There was no field of human endeavor
that he did not till with his determined hand,
that he did not sow with seeds of curiosity,
where he did not weed out lies and half-truths,
or that he did not water with a growing sense
of African awareness and heritage.
If *a book* is *a garden carried in a pocket*,
then Schomburg yielded a bumper crop,
blanketed Mount Kilimanjaro with African violets.

◆

TIME LINE

1874   January 24: Arturo Alfonso Schomburg is born in Santurce, Puerto Rico.

1891   April 17: Schomburg arrives in New York City.

1892   April 3: Schomburg is a cofounder of Las Dos Antillas, a Caribbean independence organization for which he was secretary.

Schomburg becomes a Mason, joining El Sol de Cuba Lodge no. 38, which is renamed Prince Hall Lodge no. 38.

1895   June 30: Schomburg marries Elizabeth Hatcher. They will have three sons: Maximo Gomez, Arthur Alfonso Jr., and Kingsley Guarionex.

1896   Schomburg begins teaching Spanish in New York.

1900   Elizabeth Hatcher Schomburg dies.

1901   Schomburg begins working for the New York law firm Pryor, Mellis and Harris as a messenger and clerk.

1902   March 17: Schomburg marries Elizabeth Morrow Taylor. They will have two sons: Reginald Stanfield and Nathaniel José.

1904   August: Schomburg's article "Is Hayti Decadent?" appears in *The Unique Advertiser.*

1905   January 14: The New York Public Library's 135th Street branch opens in Harlem.

1906   Schomburg takes a job in the mailroom of Bankers Trust Company. He is later promoted to a supervisor.

1911   April 9: Schomburg joins John Edward Bruce and others to establish the Negro Society for Historical Research.

1912   Schomburg coedits the *Encyclopedia of the Colored Race.*

1914   Following the death of Elizabeth Taylor Schomburg, Schomburg marries Elizabeth Green. Their family will include three children: Fernando, Dolores Marie, and Plácido Carlos.

1918   Schomburg is elected grand secretary of the Prince Hall Grand Masonic Lodge of New York.

Beginning of the Harlem Renaissance, a cultural, social, and artistic explosion.

1920   December 30: Schomburg accepts the presidency of the American Negro Academy.

1925   March: Schomburg's article "The Negro Digs Up His Past" appears in a special issue of *Survey Graphic.*

May: The 135th Street branch of the New York Public Library begins to develop the Division of Negro History, Literature and Prints.

1926   June: The Carnegie Corporation buys Schomburg's collection for $10,000 and donates it to the New York Public Library's Division of Negro History, Literature and Prints.

June–August: Schomburg travels to France, Spain, Germany, and England.

1927   January 20: The Division of Negro History, Literature and Prints at the New York Public Library's 135th Street branch opens to the public.

1930   January 1: Schomburg retires from Bankers Trust Company.

1931   Schomburg serves as curator of the Negro Collection at Fisk University Library in Nashville, Tennessee.

1932   On a trip to Cuba, Schomburg meets Cuban artists and writers and acquires materials for the New York Public Library's Division of Negro History, Literature and Prints.

1932–1938   Schomburg serves as curator of the New York Public Library's Division of Negro History, Literature, and Prints

1938   June 8: Schomburg dies in Brooklyn, New York.

1940   October: The New York Public Library's Division of Negro History, Literature and Prints is renamed the Schomburg Collection for Negro History, Literature and Prints.

1972   May: The Schomburg Collection is designated a research library of the New York Public Library and becomes the Schomburg Center for Research in Black Culture.

1980   September: A new Schomburg Center building opens, at 515 Malcolm X Boulevard in Harlem.

SOURCE NOTES

p. iii: "The American Negro . . . what slavery took away": Arthur A. Schomburg, "The Negro Digs Up His Past," *Survey Graphic* 6, no. 6 (March 1925), p. 670.

p. 1: "approach an immense . . . less inspired collector": quoted in Sinnette, p. 87.

p. 4: "Where is our historian . . . our own history?": ibid., p. 49.

p. 4: "True scholarship requires . . . done in haste": ibid., p. 32.

p. 8: "I wanted to find . . . group had contributed": ibid., p. 178.

p. 8: "book hunting disease": ibid., p. 89.

p. 10: "agitate! agitate! agitate!": Frederick Douglass, "Charges and Defense of the Free Church: An Address Delivered in Dundee, Scotland, on March 10, 1846," in Blassingame, p. 171.

p. 10: "Right is of no . . . all men are brethren": *The North Star* first edition, Maryland State Archives, The Study of the Legacy of Slavery online exhibits, http://msa.maryland.gov/msa/speccol/sc5600/sc5604/2004/december/html/north_star.html.

p. 18: "I used to lose . . . D'Artagnan, Porthos and Aramis": quoted in Sinnette, p. 14.

p. 24: "bloodhound's nose": quoted in Mooney.

p. 26: "Busy, always busy": quoted in Sinnette, p. 36.

p. 31: "There were bookshelves . . . even in the bathroom": ibid., p. 87.

p. 32: "I am proud . . . youth of my race": ibid., p. 141.

p. 32: "Include the practical . . . the present time": ibid., p. 48.

p. 38: "I depart now . . . my lost heritage": ibid., p. 145.

BIBLIOGRAPHY

Blassingame, John W., ed. *The Frederick Douglass Papers*. Vol. 1, *Speeches, Debates, and Interviews*. New Haven, CT: Yale University Press, 1979.

Mooney, Richard E. "Arthur Schomburg the Frontiersman." *New York Daily News*, June 7, 1999. http://www.nydailynews.com/archives/news/arthur-schomburg-frontiersman-article-1.833964.

Salley, Columbus. *The Black 100: A Ranking of the Most Influential Black Americans, Past and Present*. Rev. ed. Secaucus, NJ: Carol Publishing, 1999.

Schomburg Center for Research in Black Culture. *The Legacy of Arthur A. Schomburg: A Celebration of the Past, a Vision for the Future*. New York: New York Public Library/Astor, Lenox and Tilden Foundations, 1986.

Sinnette, Elinor Des Verney. *Arthur Alfonso Schomburg: Black Bibliophile and Collector*. New York: New York Public Library, 1989.

EX LIBRIS
ARTHUR A. SCHOMBURG

Schomburg placed his personal bookplate in
  every volume he collected.

It featured an engraving of an enslaved woman

in chains, hands clasped, looking heavenward.

Her plight and her plea spark questions.

Schomburg's collection holds answers:

each artifact a window on the past,

each book cover a door of possibilities,

each page a passport to freedom.